INSIDE MY HEAD

BY:JENNIFER FLAGG

WHY

Why do I sit here all
Alone?

Why do you ignore my
Calls for help?

Why does this cage keep holding
Me back?

how do I keep finding myself
In the same place time after
Time?

SCARED

The sky is closing in on me slowly
Cutting off the very air that ties
Me to life.

My heart is beginning to beat faster
And my breaths are now just shallow cries
I'm already dying and I can't
Stop this.

I see the blur of blue taking over
My eyes as my legs slowly start to
Weaken and give out.

I reach out to grab your hand to stop
From falling; I then notice that
I'm reaching into space and no one
Is there.

Why does living scare me
So much? I want to live but
I'm scared to leave this place of
Comfort and safety.

MY MIND

I live within the confines of my mind
Talking to the voices I hear every day.
The voices that isolate me from the
World around me.

When I take a step without these voices
My breath catches as if the air around
Me is contaminated.

The world is starting to spin around and
Around making me dizzy as the voices fight
To keep their hold of me.

I quickly re-track back into my mind
And close my eyes. Once again I'm back
Home to the safety and confinement of my mind.

SUMMER BREEZE

The summer breeze blows through
My long golden locks like a
Gently kiss softly floating through
The air.

As I close my eyes I can hear the summer
Breeze start to whisper to me of times
That made my heart smile.

Making me wonder how I got here to this
Place in my life. A place of chaos and insanity.
From the place of being carefree and taking
Risks without thinking of any consequences.

As I slowly open my eyes the summer breeze
Slithers away as if mocking me with it
Soft tender caress.

FIGHTING

How can I ever end this torment when
I can't stop my head and hear from
Fighting each other.

My head keeps telling me to let you go
But my heart doesn't have the strength to
Cut the strings.

I made a promise to never talk to you again and
When the next crisis happens my heart leads me
Right to your front door.

This is the last time I beg my heart to be strong
And let go for only then can I move on to
Find love once again.

NO

NO! you can't come into my heart and
Make me fall in love with you.

But you refused to give in and you walked
Right through the walls.

NO! I can't trust you with my heart because
It's been broken one to many times.

You took my hand and told me just want I wanted
To hear so I would let my guard down.

NO! I cant ever love you again because it will
Only hold me to a place and time I need to
Let go of.

There you went again refusing to listen to me
Always wanting to play the hero.

Now I know who you really are no more looking
Through the rose colored glasses. I should have
Followed my head and kept my distance from you.

PRETENDING

Every day I awake and start my chard of what
One could call a life. I paint on the happy clown
Face so no one will dare to reach further into
My soul.

Refusing to face all the pain deep in
My soul that eats at me each and
Every day. Pretending that there is nothing
In this world that can hurt me.

Pretending that your silence and lies
don't affect me at all.

Pretending I have no moments of
Weakness. I walk out the door holding my
Head high turning into someone I no
Longer know.

Pretending is my life. I no longer
Remember what reality is for I have avoided
If for so long.

All I want is to be me and put this chard away
Deep into the closet but I know there is
Only one way that will ever happen is finding
A love that is real.

BROKEN PROMISES

I remember all the things we promised
Each other on the very day you
Walked away.

Promises we made to love each other
Always and never forget that very first
Kiss that took our breath away.

But, as I watched you walk away I was
Also watching every promise we made break
One by one.

You threw our future and our love aside like
It was no better then the garbage.

Once again you played me for the fool
As you took all you could to keep surviving never
Thinking of what you were doing to me.

I know that those promises I always thought were
Broken never were because you never made them
With me.

COME BACK TO ME

I sat looking out my window every day
Praying for one last chance to see your
Smile, to hear your voice.

Always imagining what it would be like the
Day you came back to me. How it would feel to be
In your arms once again like you did so many
Times before.

Suddenly I scream out "Please come back to me!"
In hopes you hear my cries and turn back around
And come home to me.

HOLDING ON

Today I was listening to the radio when I asked
Myself a question. "why are you holding on to a love
And a man that was never what how you dreamt in
Your head?"

I couldn't come up with any real good answers
Or at least ones that would support me loving
Someone who didn't love me. The only answer I
Could come up with was that he was my safety when every
Thing else around me was falling apart.

I chose to hold on to my school girl dreams and hopes
That one day he would see just how good I was for him
And he would find his thoughts always coming back to me.

I finally realized that this was never going to happen
The way I wanted it to so that is when I knew
That I had to release those dreams of you and me
So I could move on.

EDGE OF SANITY

As I sit here today I can feel the
Edge of sanity more then I
Ever have.

I can feel the floor under me
Start to rumble as insanity
Starts to reach out for me and inches
Ever more closely.

I hear it calling me and I feel it
Reaching for me as I hold on to what is
Left of my piece of sanity.

I feel my grip slowly getting weaker
As my hunger to hold on fades. With one last
Snap and the string of sanity is broke
And I open my eyes and find that insanity has
Found me.

MY LIFE SOURCE

I can feel the very source of my
Life drain from my body drip by
Drip and its beyond my control to stop.

Let my blood fall to the ground releasing
My soul of its last breath. Slowly releasing me
To the peace I have been praying for.

I beg you to take the very last thing that
Is keeping me alive for I want to be
Without pain in my heart and soul
Once again.

HELP ME

Help me find a reason to want
To keep living.

Help me find something that I can
Believe in and hold on to.

Help me rid of all this self
Doubt that plaques my life each
Day.

Help me to find a way to surrender my heart
To love one more time.

Help me learn that there is someone in this
World I can trust my life with.

Just help me and stop watching me fall
Apart right in front of your eyes.

THE BABY

Last night in my dreams I heard
A baby crying. I sprang to my feet and
Started to run around looking for
This baby.

I then collapse as I realize there
Is no baby. Why was my mind
Playing tricks on me as I feel the tears
Fall down my face.

I just sat there for hours in the hall
With so many questions running through
My head. But as I start to pull myself off the
Ground I hear a very distinctive voice speaking
To me.

"Mommy I'm your future baby just hold
On and never give up the dream of me."

FEET

Have you ever wonders what gods though
Was when he gave us feet? And what he had planned
For them.

I have asked myself these questions over
And over. For how can something so funny
Looking be all that important.

When the answer struck me like a
Bolt of lightening. God gave us feet so
That we could walk this world and bring the
Worlds lost souls back to him.

Our feet are the most important
Part of us besides our hearts that we
Give our undying love to god. For
It will be our feet that walk us over
Heavens throne.

A FORGOTTEN ANGEL

Billy was small for a boy of eleven. So
He would always find himself being bullied
Everywhere he went. But Billy refused to let them
Win and he kept his secret close to his heart.

Billy was one of the many of children hit
By poverty. He only had the clothes on his back
And his only meals consisted of what he could
Find in the garbage can.

These days the only reason he came to school
Was for the one meal he knew he was guaranteed.
It also was one way for him to stay out of the
Freezer and warm his frostbitten
Fingers.

One day Billy no longer was
Seen around the school or school yard.
And not many people asked about him but through
The grapevine they heard that Billy had
Froze to death in the doorway of the local
Church trying to stay warm.

The people of the town started to gather
Money for this forgotten angel of eleven who
Deserved the respect of being buried.

TOUCH ME

Touch my heart like you did
For the first time all those years
Ago.

Touch me like you did on the night
You gave me a kiss that took my
Very breath away.

Touch me again like you did the first time
You held me and let all of your
Deepest secrets and feelings flow freely.

Touch me one last time to bring me back to
Life for without you all I am is just
A mere shadow.

WHERE ARE YOU?

Where have you gone? Are you safe?
Have you found someone else to love?
Or are you just running from life itself.

Why do you keep running from life has my
Loved failed you? Or do you keep running
Because you cant face your deep feelings
For me.

Where in this world are you? All you have to do
Is reach out and grab my hand for I will
Always be there for you and never
Let you down.

Where are you tonight?

ALONE

I have never felt so alone in my
Whole life as I do right now.
I wake up each morning wondering why?
What is my purpose in life.

Why is it whenever I reach out to grab
Someone's hand no one is every
There leaving me alone and in the dark
Once again.

I'm not use to living this life of
Solitude yet it has a vice grip
On me sucking all of who I
Once was.

All alone I sit here wondering when I
Will find a love that will fill this
Empty void in my soul.

Alone again to relieve my past with you
Since there will never be a future
For us.

CRYING

I sit here crying at the top of
My lungs can't you hear me? Why
Do you ignore my cries for help?

I feel the tears falling down my cheek
Yet no one has noticed me as I keep
Begging them to stop and listen.

I run to the mirror to wipe away the tears
When I see there aren't any. It's just my soul
Crying once again wondering when will it ever be
Free.

THE LIE

The last words I heard from you were
Talk to you later. As I waited to hear
From you thoughts started to race through
My mind.

Where could you be? Why don't you
Talk to me anymore? Then suddenly I felt
My heart sink.

You wrote me a letter to tell me that
You no longer love me. You didn't know how
To tell me face to face. That was because
You had been lying to me for so long
You didn't know how to tell me the
Truth.

You're caught no more need for lies
Because I will stop begging for your love
And I will move on.

THE DIFFERENCE

What makes us different? I have
Always wondered and yet that question
Refuses to leave my mind.

Is it our skin color that allows some
To make others feel less than human because
They aren't the right color.

Is it our wealth? That gives us the right
To play god when others are in
Desperate need.

Is it religion that has us fighting
in god's name?

I finally opened my eyes and realized that
There is no difference between us. We are
All the same.

DREAMING OF YOU

As I sit here dreaming of you my mind
Can't escape of the memories of
Our once perfect love.

I feel my heart beating but it's
As if I'm outside my body.
This pain I feel just feels like
An illusion.

Why is it whenever I'm alone I
Find myself going back to the memories
Of you.

Let me go and fly free so I
Can find someone I don't have
To dream about.

MY GHOSTS

I have lived in my past always
Reaching for the times that were
Refusing to see the times that
Really are.

My past has now become my present
And it takes all I have to
Wake up each morning and pretend
That I belong in this world.

I have no idea who I am without keeping
A tight grip on my past.
I need to find my present the place
That makes me safe and someplace
That will make me whole
Again.

SCARED TO LOVE

I want to give you all of my heart
And all of my soul with no
Reservations but I just don't know
If I have the strength yet.

Every time I let a piece of my heart
Open to you. You're always ready
To dig a knife in and make me
Wonder just what am I doing in this
Relationship.

My heart has been ripped and stepped
On beyond repair. It barely beats these
Days to keep me alive. Holding it back wondering
What do I really mean to you.

All you have to do is give me one good
Reason why I should give you all
Of me heart and soul without any reservations
And let my love come through.

STOLEN INNOCENCE

How could u take the one thing from
Me. The one thing I had to give
To the one that would love me body
And soul.

I kept pulling away trying to avoid the
Fate that was about to face me. But
You grabbed me and forced me to a place
I would never be able to come back from.

You played my heart and mine like a fine tuned
Instrument. Telling me everything that you though
I needed or wanted to hear just so you could
Get this part of me to break.

You took my innocence and left me there standing
With my soul naked with nothing left to hide
It from the shame.

I would have given anything to go back in time
And taken back my heart and soul
And tell that young me that I was worth so
Much more.

MY REALITY OF LOVE

I wish you could see through my eyes
How I see the reality of love.

Reality of love is breaking down and
Compromising yourself in ways you
Wished you never had.

Reality of love is grasping and
Holding on to the false hopes
And broken promises.

Reality is taking and never giving back
Or understanding what the other feels
Or needs to nourish their soul.

What has brought my thoughts of love to this
I use to think love was tender, caring, going
Beyond the limits to make sure that no matter what
There was no doubt of the love you give.

This is my jade reality of love.

A NEVERENDING DREAM

I have won and lost at love and life
But when I opened my eyes I realized
It was all a lie.. A dream I kept
Living deep within me so I never
Would have to face the truth.

A world of dreams I could go and find
Peace and safety in a world I had
No idea where I belonged.

I knew there would come a day I would have to
Face this dream would end and I would have to
Figure out what was reality and what was truth.

I have achieved things that some could only dream
To accomplish, but there isn't one day
That I ever see those achievements because I hold
On to dreams and keep running from life.

My life has been one long never ending dream and
Only now am I finding the strength to let go and allow
Myself to live life again.

MY SECRET

I have held this secret close to my heart
For so many years and I have no idea how
To let this secret out.

It's something that I know would shock everyone
If I would open up and just let my
Heart speak.. And there would be so many
Consequences to my secret but it's getting harder
To keep it hidden in the depths of my heart.

I should have let this secret out long ago when
There was a time and place I could have done
Something with this secret that I have hidden in
My heart.. Maybe I kept it hidden because I was scared
Of what would happened if it was ever revealed.

I take a deep breath and hope that this secret won't change
Things or make them uncomfortable. But if I have to hold
It any longer I know my heart would burst like a filled balloon. So
here I go, my secret is YOU, the one who made me
Smile when I had no reason to. All those years when we talked
It would bring a smile to my face who would have known
That with just one look I would see something I had missed
All those years ago. So there it's out there and everyone
Knows that you have always been my secret crush.

REACHING FOR THE TRUTH

I sit here always reaching out for something
That I can never seem to touch for every
Time my fingers get close enough to touch it
Floats farther away.

I keep reaching for the truth that I never
Known.

I long to find what I keep chasing after and finally
Find peace of mine, heart and soul but until
I find the unreachable dream I will never be able
To live my life.

I keep reaching for something that I can call
The truth just so I can move on and believe that
I have found what I have longed for all this time.

I look all around and now all I see walls moving closer
In and making me realize just how much longer there's
Left to find the truth.

I may never find the ever elusive truth that I
So long to find but maybe just maybe one day
It will find me and let me rest.

Proof

Made in the USA
Charleston, SC
02 February 2011